THE SPIRITUAL COUPLETS OF MAULANA JALALU-'D-DlN MUHAMMAD RUMI

Abridged and Translated

E.H. Whinfield

Masnavi

Book 1

[ZHINGOORA BOOKS]

THE SPIRITUAL COUPLETS
OF
MAULANA JALALU-'D-DIN MUHAMMAD RUMI

Book I.

PROLOGUE.

HEARKEN to the reed-flute, how it complains,
Lamenting its banishment from its home:
"Ever since they tore me from my osier bed,
My plaintive notes have moved men and women to tears.
I burst my breast, striving to give vent to sighs,
And to express the pangs of my yearning for my home.
He who abides far away from his home
Is ever longing for the day ho shall return.
My wailing is heard in every throng,
In concert with them that rejoice and them that weep.
Each interprets my notes in harmony with his own feelings,
But not one fathoms the secrets of my heart.
My secrets are not alien from my plaintive notes,
Yet they are not manifest to the sensual eye and ear.
Body is not veiled from soul, neither soul from body,
Yet no man hath ever seen a soul."
This plaint of the flute is fire, not mere air.
Let him who lacks this fire be accounted dead!
'Tis the fire of love that inspires the flute,1
'Tis the ferment of love that possesses the wine.
The flute is the confidant of all unhappy lovers;
Yea, its strains lay bare my inmost secrets.
Who hath seen a poison and an antidote like the flute?
Who hath seen a sympathetic consoler like the flute?
The flute tells the tale of love's bloodstained path,
It recounts the story of Majnun's love toils.
None is privy to these feelings save one distracted,
As ear inclines to the whispers of the tongue.
Through grief my days are as labor and sorrow,
My days move on, hand in hand with anguish.
Yet,, though my days vanish thus, 'tis no matter,
Do thou abide, O Incomparable Pure One! 2
But all who are not fishes are soon tired of water;
And they who lack daily bread find the day very long;
So the "Raw" comprehend not the state of the "Ripe;" 3
Therefore it behoves me to shorten my discourse.

Arise, O son! burst thy bonds and be free!
How long wilt thou be captive to silver and gold?
Though thou pour the ocean into thy pitcher,
It can hold no more than one day's store.
The pitcher of the desire of the covetous never fills,
The oyster-shell fills not with pearls till it is content;
Only he whose garment is rent by the violence of love
Is wholly pure from covetousness and sin.
Hail to thee, then, O LOVE, sweet madness!
Thou who healest all our infirmities!
Who art the physician of our pride and self-conceit!
Who art our Plato and our Galen!
Love exalts our earthly bodies to heaven,
And makes the very hills to dance with joy!
O lover, 'twas love that gave life to Mount Sinai, 4
When "it quaked, and Moses fell down in a swoon."
Did my Beloved only touch me with his lips,
I too, like the flute, would burst out in melody.
But he who is parted from them that speak his tongue,
Though he possess a hundred voices, is perforce dumb.
When the rose has faded and the garden is withered,
The song of the nightingale is no longer to be heard.
The BELOVED is all in all, the lover only veils Him; 5
The BELOVED is all that lives, the lover a dead thing.
When the lover feels no longer LOVE's quickening,
He becomes like a bird who has lost its wings. Alas!
How can I retain my senses about me,
When the BELOVED shows not the light of His countenance?
LOVE desires that this secret should be revealed,
For if a mirror reflects not, of what use is it?
Knowest thou why thy mirror reflects not?
Because the rust has not been scoured from its face.
If it were purified from all rust and defilement,
It would reflect the shining of the SUN Of GOD.6
O friends, ye have now heard this tale,
Which sets forth the very essence of my case.
*NOTES:
1. Love signifies the strong attraction that draws all creatures back to
reunion with their Creator.

2. Self-annihilation leads to eternal life in God the universal Noumenon, by whom all phenomena subsist. See Gulshan i Raz, I. 400.

3. "Raw" and "Ripe" are terms for "Men of externals" and "Men of heart" or Mystics.

4. Alluding to the giving of the law on Mount Sinai. Koran vii. 139.

5. All phenomenal existences (man included) are but "veils" obscuring the face of the Divine Noumenon, the only real existence, and the moment His sustaining presence is withdrawn they at once relapse into their original nothingness. See Gulshan i Raz, I. 165.

6. So Bernard of Clairvaux. See Gulshan i Raz, I. 435.

STORY I.

The Prince and the Handmaid.
A prince, while engaged on a hunting excursion, espied a fair maiden, and by promises of gold induced her to accompany him. After a time she fell sick, and the prince had her tended by divers physicians. As, however, they all omitted to say, "God willing,1 we will cure her," their treatment was of no avail. So the prince offered prayer, and in answer thereto a physician was sent from heaven. He at once condemned his predecessors' view of the case, and by a very skilful diagnosis, discovered that the real cause of the maiden's illness was her love for a certain goldsmith of Samarcand. In accordance with the physician's advice, the prince sent to Samarcand and fetched the goldsmith, and married him to the lovesick maiden, and for six months the pair lived together in the utmost harmony and happiness. At the end of that period the physician, by divine command, gave the goldsmith a poisonous draught, which caused his strength and beauty to decay, and he then lost favour with the maiden, and she was reunited to the king. This Divine command was precisely similar to God's command to Abraham to slay his son Ishmael, and to the act of the angel in slaying the servant of Moses,2 and is therefore beyond human criticism.
Description of Love.
A true lover is proved such by his pain of heart;
No sickness is there like sickness of heart.
The lover's ailment is different from all ailments;
Love is the astrolabe of God's mysteries.
A lover may hanker after this love or that love,
But at the last he is drawn to the KING of love.
However much we describe and explain love,
When we fall in love we are ashamed of our words.
Explanation by the tongue makes most things clear,
But love unexplained is clearer.
When pen hasted to write,
On reaching the subject of love it split in twain.
When the discourse touched on the matter of love,
Pen was broken and paper torn.
In explaining it Reason sticks fast, as an ass in mire;

Naught but Love itself can explain love and lovers!
None but the sun can display the sun,
If you would see it displayed, turn not away from it.
Shadows, indeed, may indicate the sun's presence,
But only the sun displays the light of life.
Shadows induce slumber, like evening talks,
But when the sun arises the "moon is split asunder." 3
In the world there is naught so wondrous as the sun,
But the Sun of the soul sets not and has no yesterday.
Though the material sun is unique and single,
We can conceive similar suns like to it.
But the Sun of the soul, beyond this firmament,
No like thereof is seen in concrete or abstract.4
Where is there room in conception for His essence,
So that similitudes of HIM should be conceivable?
Shamsu-'d-Din of Tabriz importunes Jalalu-'d-Din
to compose the Masnavi.
The sun (Shams) of Tabriz is a perfect light,
A sun, yea, one of the beams of God!
When the praise was heard of the "Sun of Tabriz,"
The sun of the fourth heaven bowed its head.
Now that I have mentioned his name, it is but right
To set forth some indications of his beneficence.
That precious Soul caught my skirt,
Smelling the perfume of the garment of Yusuf;
And said, "For the sake of our ancient friendship,
Tell forth a hint of those sweet states of ecstasy,
That earth and heaven may be rejoiced,
And also Reason and Spirit, a hundredfold."
I said, "O thou who art far from 'The Friend,'
Like a sick man who has strayed from his physician,
Importune me not, for I am beside myself;
My understanding is gone, I cannot sing praises.
Whatsoever one says, whose reason is thus astray,
Let him not boast; his efforts are useless.
Whatever he says is not to the point,
And is clearly inapt and wide of the mark.
What can I say when not a nerve of mine is sensible?
Can I explain 'The Friend' to one to whom He is no Friend?

Verily my singing His praise were dispraise,
For 'twould prove me existent, and existence is error.5
Can I describe my separation and my bleeding heart?
Nay, put off this matter till another season."
He said, " Feed me, for I am an hungered,
And at once, for 'the time is a sharp sword.'
O comrade, the Sufi is 'the son of time present.' 6
It is not the rule of his canon to say, 'To-morrow.'
Can it be that thou art not a true Sufi?
Ready money is lost by giving credit."
I said, "'Tis best to veil the secrets of 'The Friend.'
So give good heed to the morals of these stories.
That is better than that the secrets of 'The Friend'
Should be noised abroad in the talk of strangers."
He said, "Without veil or covering or deception,
Speak out, and vex me not, O man of many words!
Strip off the veil and speak out, for do not I
Enter under the same coverlet as the Beloved?"
I said, "If the Beloved were exposed to outward view,
Neither wouldst thou endure, nor embrace, nor form.
Press thy suit, yet with moderation;
A blade of grass cannot, pierce a mountain.
If the sun that illumines the world
Were to draw nigher, the world would be consumed.7
Close thy mouth and shut the eyes of this matter,
That, the world's life be not made a bleeding heart.
No longer seek this peril, this bloodshed;
Hereafter impose silence on the 'Sun of Tabriz.'"
He said, "Thy words are endless. Now tell forth
All thy story from its beginning."
*NOTES:
1. As enjoined in Koran xviii. 23. One cannot converse with a strict
Mosalman for five minutes without hearing the formula, "In sha
Allah Ta'alla," or D. V.
2. Koran xviii. 73.
3. Koran liv. I.
4. There is a tradition, "I know my Lord by my Lord."
5. See Gulshan i Raz, I. 400. In the state of union self remains not.
6. The Sufi is the "son of the time present," because he is an

Energumen, or passive instrument moved by the divine impulse of the moment. "The time present is a sharp sword," because the divine impulse of the moment dominates the Energumen, and executes its decrees sharply. See Sohravardi quoted in Notices et Extraits des MSS., xii. 371 note.

7. "When its Lord appears in glory to the Mount of existence, Existence is laid low, like the dust of the road." Gulshan i Raz, I. 195.

STORY II.

The Oilman and his Parrot.
An oilman possessed a parrot which used to amuse him with its
agreeable prattle, and to watch his shop when he went out. One day,
when the parrot was alone in the shop, a cat upset one of the oil-jars.
When the oilman returned home he thought that the parrot had
done this mischief, and in his anger he smote the parrot such a blow
on the head as made all its feathers drop off, and so stunned it that it
lost the power of speech for several days. But one day the parrot saw
a bald-headed man passing the shop, and recovering its speech, it
cried out, "Pray, whose oil-jar did you upset?" The passers-by smiled
at the parrot's mistake in confounding baldness caused by age with
the loss of its own feathers due to a blow.
Confusion of saints with hypocrites.
Worldly senses are the ladder of earth,
Spiritual senses are the ladder of heaven.
The health of the former is sought of the leech,
The health of the latter from "The Friend."
The health of the former arises from tending the body,
That of the latter from mortifying the flesh.
The kingly soul lays waste the body,
And after its destruction he builds it anew.
Happy the soul who for love of God
Has lavished family, wealth, and goods!
Has destroyed its house to find the hidden treasure,
And with that treasure has rebuilt it in fairer sort;
Has dammed up the stream and cleansed the channel,
And then turned a fresh stream into. the channel;
Has cut its flesh to extract a spear-head,1
Causing a fresh skin to grow again over the wound;
Has razed the fort to oust, the infidel in possession,
And then rebuilt it with a hundred towers and bulwarks.
Who can describe the unique work of Grace?
I have been forced to illustrate it by these similes.

Sometimes it presents one appearance, sometimes another.
Yea, the affair of religion is only bewilderment.
Not, such as occurs when one turns one's back on God,
But such as when one is drowned and absorbed in Him.
The latter has his face ever turned to God,
The former's face shows his undisciplined self-will.
Watch the face of each one, regard it well,
It may be by serving thou wilt recognize Truth's face.
As there are many demons with men's faces,
It is wrong to join hand with every one.
When the fowler sounds his decoy whistle,
That the birds may be beguiled by that snare,
The birds hear that call simulating a bird's call,
And, descending from the air, find net and knife.
So vile hypocrites steal the language of Darveshes,
In order to beguile the simple with their trickery.
The works of the righteous are light and heat,
The works of the evil treachery and shamelessness.
They make stuffed lions to scare the simple,
They give the title of Muhammad to false Musailima.
But Musailma retained the name of "Liar,"
And Muhammad that of "Sublimest of beings."
That wine of God (the righteous) yields a perfume of musk;
Other wine (the evil) is reserved for penalties and pains.
*NOTES:
1. These are all figures and types of self-annihilation in order to the
acquisition of eternal life in God.

STORY III.

The Jewish King, his Vazir, and the Christians.
A certain Jewish king used to persecute the Christians, desiring to exterminate their faith. His Vazir persuaded him to try a stratagem, namely, to mutilate the Vazir himself, and expel him from his court, with the intent that he might take refuge with the Christians, and stir up mutual dissensions amongst them. The Vazir's suggestion was adopted.1 He fled to the Christians, and found no difficulty in persuading them that he had been treated in that barbarous way on account of his attachment to the Christian faith. He soon gained complete influence over them, and was accepted as a saintly martyr and a divine teacher. Only a few discerning men divined his treachery ; the majority were all deluded by him. The Christians were divided into twelve legions, and at the head of each was a captain. To each of these captains the Vazir gave secretly a volume of religious directions, taking care to make the directions in each volume different from and contradictory to those in the others. One volume enjoined fasting, another charity, another faith, another works, and so on. Afterwards the Vazir withdrew into a cave, and refused to come out to instruct his disciples, in spite of all their entreaties. Calling the captains to him, he gave secret instructions to each to set himself up as his successor, and to be guided by the instructions in the volume secretly confided to him, and to slay all other claimants of the apostolic office. Having given these directions, he slew himself. In the event each captain set himself up as the Vazir's successor, and the Christians were split up into many sects at enmity with one another, even as the Vazir had intended. But the malicious scheme did not, altogether succeed, as one faithful band cleaved to the name of "Ahmad," mentioned in the Gospel,2 and were thus saved from sharing the ruin of the rest.
The Vazir's Teaching.
Myriads of Christians flocked round him,
One after another they assembled in his street.
Then he would preach to them of mysteries,
Mysteries of the Gospel, of stoles, of prayers.
He would preach to them with eloquent words

Concerning the words and acts of the Messiah.
Outwardly he was a preacher of religious duties,
But within a decoy call and a fowler's snare.
Therefore the followers of the Prophet ('Isa)
Were beguiled by the fraud of that demon soul.
He mingled in his discourses many secret doctrines
Concerning devotion and sincerity of soul.
He taught them to make a fair show of devotion,
But to say of secret sins, "What do they matter?"
Hair by hair and jot by jot they learned of him
Fraud of soul, as roses might learn of garlic.
Hair-splitters and all their disciples
Are darkened by similar preaching and discourse.
The Christians gave their hearts to him entirely,
For the blind faith of the vulgar has no discernment.
In their inmost breasts they planted love of him,
And fancied him to be the Vicar of Christ;
Yea, him, that one-eyed and cursed Dajjal! 3
Save us. O God ! who art our only defender!
O God, there are hundreds of snares and baits,
And we are even as greedy and foolish birds;
Every moment our feet are caught in a fresh snare ;
Yea, each one of us, though he be a falcon or Simurgh!
Thou dost release us every moment, and straightway
We again fly into the snare, O Almighty One!
Sleep of the body the soul's awakening.
Every night Thou freest our spirits from the body
And its snare, making them pure as rased tablets.
Every night spirits are released from this cage,
And set free, neither lording it nor lorded over.
At night prisoners are unaware of their prison,
At night kings are unaware of their majesty.
Then there is no thought or care for loss or gain,
No regard to such an one or such an one.
The state of the "Knower" is such as this, even when awake.
God says,4 "Thou wouldst deem him awake though asleep,
Sleeping to the affairs of the world, day and night,
Like a pen in the directing hand of the writer.
He who sees not the hand which effects the writing

Fancies the effect proceeds from the motion of the pen.
If the "Knower" revealed the particulars of this state,
'Twould rob the vulgar of their sensual sleep.
His soul wanders in the desert that has no similitude;
Like his body, his spirit is enjoying perfect rest;
Freed from desire of eating and drinking,
Like a bird escaped from cage and snare.
But when he is again beguiled into the snare,
He cries for help to the Almighty.
Laila and the Khalifa.
The Khalifa said to Laila, "Art thou really she
For whom Majnun lost his head and went distracted?
Thou art not fairer than many other fair ones."
She replied, "Be silent; thou art not Majnun!"
If thou hadst Majnun's eyes,
The two worlds would be within thy view.
Thou art in thy senses, but Majnun is beside himself.
In love to be wide awake is treason.
The more a man is awake, the more he sleeps (to love);
His (critical) wakefulness is worse than slumbering.
Our wakefulness fetters our spirits,
Then our souls are a prey to divers whims,
Thoughts of loss and gain and fears of misery.
They retain not purity, nor dignity, nor lustre,
Nor aspiration to soar heavenwards.
That one is really sleeping who hankers after each whim
And holds parley with each fancy.
The twelve volumes of theology.

He drew up a separate scroll to the address of each,
The contents of each scroll of a different tenor;
The rules of each of a different purport,
This contradictory of that, from beginning to end.
In one the road of fasting and asceticism
Was made the pillar and condition of right devotion.
In one 'twas said, "Abstinence profits not;

Sincerity in this path is naught but charity."
In one 'twas said, "Thy fasting and thy charity
Are both a making thyself equal with God;
Save faith and utter resignation to God's will
In weal and woe, all virtues are fraud and snares."
In one 'twas said, "Works are the one thing needful;
The doctrine of faith without works is a delusion."
In one 'twas said, "Commands and prohibitions are
Not for observance, but to demonstrate our weakness,
That we may see our own weakness (to carry them out),
And thereby recognize and confess God's power." 5
In one 'twas said, "Reference to thine own weakness
Is ingratitude for God's mercies towards us.
Rather regard thy power, for thou hast power from God.
Know thy power to be God's grace, for 'tis of Him."
In one 'twas said, "Leave power and weakness alone;
Whatever withdraws thine eyes from God is an idol."
In one 'twas said, "Quench not thy earthy torch,6
That it may be a light to lighten mankind.
If thou neglectest regard and care for it,
Thou wilt quench at midnight the lamp of union."
In one 'twas said, "Quench that torch without fear,
That in lieu of one thou may'st see a thousand joys,
For by quenching the light the soul is rejoiced,
And thy Laila is then as bold as her Majnun.
Whoso to display his devotion renounces the world,
The world is ever with him, before and behind."
In one 'twas said, "Whatsoever God has given thee
In His creation, that He has made sweet to thee;
Yea, pleasant to thee and allowable. Take it, then,
And cast not thyself into the pangs of abstinence."
In one 'twas said, "Give up all thou possessest,
For to be ruled by covetousness is grievous sin."
(Ah! how many diverse roads are pointed out,
And each followed by some sect for dear life!
If the right road were easily attainable,
Every Jew and Gueber would have hit on it!)
In one 'twas said, "The right road is attainable,
For the heart's life is the food of the soul.

Whatever is enjoyed by the carnal man
Yields no fruit, even as salt and waste land.
Its result is naught but remorse,
Its traffic yields only loss.
It is not profitable in the long run;
Its name is called 'bankrupt' in the upshot.
Discern, then, the bankrupt from the profitable,
Consider the eventual value of this and that."
In one 'twas said, "Choose ye a wise Director,
But foresight of results is not found in dignities."
(Each sect looked to results in a different way,
And so, perforce, became captive to errors.
Real foresight of results is not simple jugglery,
Otherwise all these differences would not have arisen.
In one 'twas said, "Thyself art thy master,
Inasmuch as thou art acquainted with the Master of all;
Be a man, and not another man's beast of burden!
Follow thine own way and lose not thy head!"
In one 'twas said, "All we see is One.
Whoever says 'tis two is suffering from double vision."
In one 'twas said, "A hundred are even as one."7
But whoso thinks this is a. madman.
Each scroll had its contrary piece of rhetoric,
In form and substance utterly opposed to it;
This contrary to that, from first to last,
As if each was compounded of poison and antidotes.

*NOTES:
1. Compare the story of Zopyrus, Herodotus, iii. 155.
2. John xiv. 26: "But the Comforter (parakletos) shall teach you all
things." Mosalmans read periklytos, "praised" = Muhammad.
3. Dajjal, i.e., Antichrist. Sale, Prelim. Discourse, p. 57.
4. Said of the Seven Sleepers in the cave. Koran xviii. 17; "Knower" =
the Gnostic who through ecstasy beholds divine verities.
5. This was the doctrine of the Jabriyan or extreme predestinarians.
6. i.e.. Hide not thy light (of good works or of self-denial) under a
bushel.
7. Alluding to the doctrine of the Trinity.

STORY IV.

Another Tyrannical Jewish King.

A certain Jewish king, the same who is referred to in the Sura "Signs of the Zodiac," I made up his mind to utterly exterminate the Christian faith, and with that view he set up a huge idol, and issued commands that all who refused to worship it should be cast into the fire. Thereupon his officers seized a Christian woman with her babe, and as she refused to worship it, they cast the babe into the fire. But the babe cried out to its mother, "Be not afraid, the fire has no power to burn me; it is as cool as water!" Hearing this, the rest of the Christians leapt into the fire, and found that it did not burn them. The king reproached the fire for failing to do its office, but the fire replied that it was God's servant, and that its consuming properties were not to be used for evil purposes. It then blazed up and consumed the king, and all his Jews with him.

Second causes only operate in subordination to,
and form the impulsion of, the First Cause.
Air, earth, water, and fire are God's servants.
To us they seem lifeless, but to God living.
In God's presence fire ever waits to do its service,
Like a submissive lover with no will of its own.
When you strike steel on flint fire leaps forth;
But 'tis by God's command it thus steps forth.
Strike not together the flint and steel of wrong,
For the pair will generate more, like man and woman.
The flint and steel are themselves causes, yet
Look higher for the First Cause, O righteous man!
For that Cause precedes this second cause.
How can a cause exist of itself without precedent cause?
That Cause makes this cause operative,
And again helpless and inoperative.
That Cause, which is a guiding light to the prophets,
That, I say, is higher than these second causes.
Men's minds recognize these second causes,
But only prophets perceive the action of the First Cause.
Praise compared to vapour drawn upwards,
and then descending in rain.

Though water be enclosed in a reservoir,
Yet air will absorb it, for 'tis its supporter;
It sets it free and bears it to its source,
Little by little, so that you see not the process.
In like manner this breath of ours by degrees
Steals away our souls from the prison-house of earth.
" The good word riseth up to Him,"2
Rising from us whither He knoweth.
Our breathings are lifted up in fear of God,
Offerings from us to the throne of Eternity.
Then come down to us rewards for our praises,
The double thereof, yea, mercies from the King of Glory.
Therefore are we constrained to utter these praises
That slaves may attain the height of God's gifts.
And so this rising and descent go on evermore,
And cease not forever and aye.
To speak in plain Persian, this attraction
Comes from the same quarter whence comes this sweet savour.3

*NOTES:
1. Koran lxxxv.
2. Koran, xxxv. II.
3. Sweet savour, i.e., the joy of heart experienced by the offerer of
prayer when his prayer is accepted of God. See Book II. Story XVII.

STORY V.

The Lion and the Beasts.
In the book of Kalila and Damna a story is told of a lion who held all
the beasts of the neighborhood in subjection, and was in the habit of
making constant raids upon them, to take and kill such of them as he
required for his daily food. At last the beasts took counsel together,
and agreed to deliver up one of their company every day, to satisfy
the lion's hunger, if he, on his part, would cease to annoy them by
his continual forays. The lion was at first unwilling to trust to their
promise, remarking that he always preferred to rely on his own
exertions; but the beasts succeeded in persuading him that he would
do well to trust Providence and their word. To illustrate the thesis
that human exertions are vain, they related a story of a man who got
Solomon to transport him to Hindustan to escape the angel of death,
but was smitten by the angel the moment he got there. Having
carried their point, the beasts continued for some time to perform
their engagement. One day it came to the turn of the hare to be
delivered up as a victim to the lion; but he requested the others to let
him practice a stratagem. They scoffed at him, asking how such silly
beast as he could pretend to outwit the lion. The hare assured them
that wisdom was of God, and God might choose weak things to
confound the strong. At last they consented to let him try his luck.
He took his way slowly to the lion, and found him sorely enraged. In
excuse for his tardy arrival he represented that he and another hare
had set out together to appear before the lion, but a strange lion had
seized the second hare, and carried it off in spite of his
remonstrances. On hearing this, the lion was exceeding wroth, and
commanded the hare to show him the foe who had trespassed on his
preserves. Pretending to be afraid, the hare got the lion to take him
upon his back, and directed him to a well. On looking down the
well, the lion saw in the water the reflection of himself and of the
hare on his back; and thinking that he saw his foe with the stolen
hare, he plunged in to attack him, and was drowned, while the hare
sprang off his back and escaped. This folly on the part, of the lion
was predestined to punish him for denying God's ruling providence.
So Adam, though he knew the names of all things, in accordance
with God's predestination, neglected to obey a single prohibition,

19

and his disobedience cost him dearly.
Trust in God, as opposed to human exertions.
The beasts said, "O enlightened sage,
Lay aside caution; it cannot help thee against destiny;
To worry with precaution is toil and moil;
Go, trust in Providence, trust is the better part.
War not with the divine decree, O hot-headed one,
Lest that decree enter into conflict with thee.
Man should be as dead before the commands of God
Lest a blow befall him from the Lord of all creatures."
He said, "True; but though trust be our mainstay,
Yet the Prophet teaches us to have regard to means.
The Prophet cried with a loud voice,
'Trust in God, yet tie the camel's leg.' 1
Hear the adage, 'The worker is the friend of God;'2
Through trust in Providence neglect not to use means.
Go, O Quietists, practice trust with self-exertion,
Exert yourself to attain your objects, bit by bit.
In order to succeed, strive and exert yourselves;
If ye strive not for your objects, ye are fools."
They said, "What is gained from the poor by exertions
Is a fraudulent morsel that will bring ill luck.
Again, know that self-exertion springs from weakness;
Relying on other means is a blot upon perfect trust.
Self-exertion is not more noble than trust in God.
What is more lovely than committing oneself to God?
Many there are who flee from one danger to a worse;
Many flee from a snake and meet a dragon.
Man plans a stratagem, and thereby snares himself;
What he takes for life turns out, to be destruction.
He shuts the door after his foe is in the house.
After this sort were the schemes of Pharaoh.
That jealous king slew a myriad babes,
While Moses, whom he sought, was in his house.
Our eyes are subject to many infirmities;
Go! annihilate your sight in God's sight.
For our foresight His foresight is a fair exchange;
In His sight is all that ye can desire.
So long as a babe cannot grasp or run,

It takes its father's back for its carriage.
But when it becomes independent and uses its hands,
It falls into grievous troubles and disgrace.
The souls of our first parents, even before their hands,
Flew away from fidelity after vain pleasure.
Being made captives by the command, 'Get down hence,' 3
They became bond-slaves of enmity, lust, and vanity.
We are the family of the Lord and His sucking babes.
The Prophet said, 'The people are God's family;'
He who sends forth the rain from heaven,
Can He not also provide us our daily bread?"
The lion said, "True; yet the Lord of creatures
Sets a ladder before our feet.
Step by step must we mount up to the roof!
The notion of fatalism is groundless in this place.
Ye have feet why then pretend ye are lame?
Ye have hands why then conceal your claws?
When a master places a spade in the hand of a slave,
The slave knows his meaning without being told.
Like this spade, our hands are our Master's hints to us;
Yea, if ye consider, they are His directions to us.
When ye have taken to heart His hints,
Ye will shape your life in reliance on their direction;
Wherefore these hints disclose His intent,
Take the burden from you, and appoint your work.
He that bears it makes it bearable by you,
He that is able makes it within your ability.
Accept His command, and you will be able to execute it;
Seek union with Him, and you will find yourselves united.
Exertion is giving thanks for God's blessings;
Think ye that your fatalism gives such thanks?
Giving thanks for blessings increases blessings,
But fatalism snatches those blessings from your hands.
Your fatalism is to sleep on the road; sleep not
Till ye behold the gates of the King's palace.
Ah! sleep not, O unreflecting fatalists,
Till ye have reached that fruit-laden Tree of Life
Whose branches are ever shaken by the wind,
And whose fruit is showered on the sleepers' heads.

Fatalism means sleeping amidst highwaymen.
Can a cock who crows too soon expect peace?
If ye cavil at and accept not God's hints,
Though ye count yourselves men, see, ye are women.
The quantum of reason ye possessed is lost,
And the head whose reason has fled is a tail.
Inasmuch as the unthankful are despicable,
They are at last cast into the fiery pit.
If ye really have trust in God, exert yourselves,
And strive, in constant reliance on the Almighty."
Wisdom is granted often times to the weak.
He said, "O friends, God has given me inspiration.
Often times strong counsel is suggested to the weak.
The wit taught by God to the bee
Is withheld from the lion and the wild ass.
It fills its cells with liquid sweets,
For God opens the door of this knowledge to it.
The skill taught by God to the silkworm
Is a learning beyond the reach of the elephant.
The earthly Adam was taught of God names, 4
So that his glory reached the seventh heaven.
He laid low the name and fame of the angels, 5
Yet blind indeed are they whom God dooms to doubt!
The devotee of seven hundred thousand years (Satan)
Was made a muzzle for that yearling calf (Adam), 6
Lest he should suck milk of the knowledge of faith,
And soar on high even to the towers of heaven.
The knowledge of men of external sense is a muzzle
To stop them sucking milk of that sublime knowledge.
But God drops into the heart a single pearl-drop
Which is not bestowed on oceans or skies!"
"How long regard ye mere form, O form-worshippers?
Your souls, void of substance, rest still in forms.
If the form of man were all that made man,
Ahmad and Abu Jahl would be upon a par.
A painting on a wall resembles a man,
But see what it is lacking in that empty form.
'Tis life that is lacking to that mere semblance of man.
Go! seek for that pearl it never will find.

The heads of earth's lions were bowed down
When God gave might to the Seven Sleepers' dog. 7
What mattered its despised form
When its soul was drowned in the sea of light?"
Human wisdom, the manifestation of divine.
On his way to the lion the hare lingered,
Devising a stratagem with himself.
He proceeded on his way after delaying long,
In order to have a secret or two for the lion.
What worlds the principle of Reason embraces!
How broad is this ocean of Reason!
Yea, the Reason of man is a boundless ocean.
O son, that ocean requires, as it were, a diver. 8
On this fair ocean our human forms
Float about, like bowls on the surface of water;
Yea like cups on the surface, till they are. filled;
And when filled, these cups sink into the water.
The ocean of Reason is not seen ; reasoning men are seen;
But our forms (minds) are only as waves or spray thereof.
Whatever form that ocean uses as its instrument,
Therewith it casts its spray far and wide. 9
Till the heart sees the Giver of the secret,
Till it espies that Bowman shooting from afar,
It fancies its own steed lost, while in bewilderment
It is urging that steed hither and thither; 10
It fancies its own steed lost, when all the while
That swift steed is bearing it on like the wind.
In deep distress that blunder head
Runs from door to door, searching and inquiring,
"Who and where is he that hath stolen my steed?"
They say, "What is this thou ridest on, O master?"
He says, "True, 'tis a steed; but where is mine?"
They say, "Look to thyself, O rider; thy steed is there."
The real Soul is lost to view, and seems far off; 11
Thou art like a pitcher with full belly but dry lip;
How canst thou ever see red, green, and scarlet
Unless thou seest the light first of all?
When thy sight is dazzled by colors,
These colors veil the light from thee.

But when night veils those colors from thee,
Thou seest that colors are seen only through light.
As there is no seeing outward colors without light,
So it is with the mental colors within.
Outward colors arise from the light of sun and stars,
And inward colors from the Light on high.
The light that lights the eye is also the heart's Light;
The eye's light proceeds from the Light of the heart.
But the light that lights the heart is the Light of God,
Which is distinct from the light of reason and sense.
At night there is no light, and colors are not seen;
Hence we know what light is by its opposite, darkness.
At night no colors are visible, for light is lacking.
How can color be the attribute of dark blackness?
Looking on light is the same as looking on colors;
Opposite shows up opposite, as a Frank a Negro.
The opposite of light shows what is light,
Hence colors too are known by their opposite.
God created pain and grief for this purpose,
To wit, to manifest happiness by its opposites. 12
Hidden things are manifested by their opposites;
But, as God has no opposite. He remains hidden.
God's light has no opposite in the range of creation
Whereby it may be manifested to view.
Perforce "Our eyes see not Him, though He sees us." 13
Behold this in the case of Moses and Mount Sinai. 14
Discern form from substance, as lion from desert,
Or as sound and speech from the thought they convey.
The sound and speech arise from the thought;
Thou knowest not where is the Ocean of thought;
Yet when thou seest fair waves of speech,
Thou knowest there is a glorious Ocean beneath them.
When waves of thought arise from the Ocean of Wisdom,
They assume the forms of sound and speech.
These forms of speech are born and die again,
These wa,ves cast themselves back into the Ocean.
Form is born of That which is without form,
And goes again, for, "Verily to Him do we return." 15
Wherefore to thee every moment come death and "return."

Mustafa saith, "The world endureth only a moment."
So, thought is an arrow shot by God into the air.
How can it stay in the air? It returns to God.
Every moment the world and we are renewed, 16
Yet we are ignorant of this renewing forever and aye.
Life, like a stream of water, is renewed and renewed,
Though it wears the appearance of continuity in form.
That seeming continuity arises from its swift renewal,
As when a single spark of fire is whirled round swiftly. 17
If a single spark be whirled round swiftly,
It seems to the eye a continuous line of fire.
This apparent extension, owing to the quick motion,
Demonstrates the rapidity with which it is moved.
If ye seek the deepest student of this mystery,
Lo! 'tis Husamu-'d-Din, the most exalted of creatures!
*NOTES:
1. "Trust in God and keep your powder dry."
2. "Laborare est orare."
3. Koran ii. 341.
4. "And He taught Adam the names of all things" (Koran ii. 29).
5. The angels said, "We have no knowledge but what thou hast given us to know" (Koran ii. 30).
6. See Gulshan i Raz, I. 543.
7. Koran xviii. 17.
8. See Gulshan i Raz, I. 575: The ocean of Reason is the same as what is elsewhere called the ocean of Being, viz., the Noumenon, or Divine substratum of all phenomenal being and thought.
9. "Those arrows were God's, not yours" (Koran viii. 17); i.e., Man's reason proceeds from God, the "Only Real Agent."
10. Alluding to the "Believer's lost camel " (Book II. Story XII., infra.). Men seek wisdom, and do not know that in themselves is the reflected wisdom of God (Gulshan i Raz, I. 435).
11. The real Soul, i.e., the spirit which God "breathed into man" (Koran xv. 29). "In yourselves are signs; will ye not behold them?" (Koran li, 21).
12. See Gulshan i Raz, I. 92. Mr. Mansel (Bampton Lectures, p. 49) says: "A thing can be known as that which it is only by being distinguished from that which it is not." But the Infinite Deity ex hypothesi includes all things; so there is nothing to contrast Him

25

with.

13. Koran vi. 103.

14. Koran vii. 139: "He said, 'Thou shalt not see me.'"

15. Koran ii. 151.

16. See Gulshan i Raz, I. 645: All phenomena are every moment renewed by fresh effluxes of being from the Divine Noumenon.

17. See Gulshan i Raz, I. 710.

STORY VI.

Omar and the Ambassador.
The hare, having delivered his companions from the tyranny of the
lion, in the manner just described, proceeds to improve the occasion
by exhorting them to engage in a greater and more arduous warfare,
viz., the struggle against their inward enemy, the lusts of the flesh.
He illustrates his meaning by the story of an ambassador who was
sent by the Emperor of Rum to the Khalifa 'Omar. On approaching
Medina this ambassador inquired for 'Omar's palace, and learned
that 'Omar dwelt in no material palace, but in a spiritual tabernacle,
only visible to purified hearts. At last he discerned 'Omar lying
under a palm-tree, and drew near to him in fear and awe. 'Omar
received him kindly, and instructed him in the doctrine of the
mystical union with God. The ambassador heard him gladly, and
asked him two questions, first, How can souls descend from heaven
to earth? and secondly, With what object are souls imprisoned in the
bonds of flesh and blood? 'Omar responded, and the ambassador
accepted his teaching, and became a pure-hearted Sufi. The hare
urged his companions to abjure lust and pride, and to go and do
likewise.
God's agency reconciled with man's freewill.
The ambassador said, "O Commander of the faithful,
How comes the soul down from above to earth?
How can so noble a bird be confined in a cage?"
He said, "God speaks words of power to souls,
To things of naught, without eyes or ears,
And at these words they all spring into motion;
At His words of power these nothings arise quickly,
And strong impulse urges them into existence.
Again, He speaks other spells to these creatures,
And swiftly drives them back again into Not-being.
He speaks to the rose's ear, and causes it to bloom;
He speaks to the tulip, and makes it blossom.
He speaks a spell to body, and it becomes soul;
He speaks to the sun, and it becomes a fount of light.
Again, in its ear He whispers a word of power,
And its face is darkened as by a hundred eclipses.

What is it that God says to the ear of earth,
That it attends thereto and rests steadfast?
What is it that Speaker says to the cloud,
That it pours forth rain-water like a water-skin?
Whosoever is bewildered by wavering will, 1
In his ear hath God whispered His riddle,
That He may bind him on the horns of a dilemma;
For he says, 'Shall I do this or its reverse?'
Also from God comes the preference of one alternative;
'Tis from God's impulsion that man chooses one of the two.
If you desire sanity in this embarrassment,
Stuff not the ear of your mind with cotton.
Take the cotton of evil suggestions from the mind's ear, 2
That the heavenly voice from above may enter it,
That you may understand that riddle of His,
That you may be cognisant of that open secret.
Then the mind's ear becomes the sensorium of inspiration;
For what is this Divine voice but the inward voice? 3
The spirit's eye and ear possess this sense,
The eye and ear of reason and sense lack it.
The word 'compulsion' makes me impatient for love's sake;
'Tis he who loves not who is fettered by compulsion.
This is close communion with God, not compulsion,
The shining of the sun, and not a dark cloud.
Or, if it be compulsion, 'tis not common compulsion,
It is not the domination of wanton wilfulness.
O son, they understand this compulsion
For whom God opens the eyes of the inner man.
Things hidden and things future are plain to them;
To speak of the past seems to them despicable.
They possess freewill and compulsion besides, 4
As in oyster-shells raindrops are pearls.
Outside the shell they are raindrops, great and small;
Inside they are precious pearls, big and little.
These men also resemble the musk deer's bag;
Outside it is blood, but inside pure musk;
Yet, say not that outside 'twas mere blood,
Which on entering the bag becomes musk.
Nor say that outside the alembic 'twas mere copper,

And becomes gold inside, when mixed with elixir.
In you freewill and compulsion are vain fancies,
But in them they are the light of Almighty power.
On the table bread is a mere lifeless thing,
When taken into the body it is a life-giving spirit.
This transmutation occurs not in the table's heart,
'Tis soul effects this transmutation with water of life.
Such is the power of the soul, O man of right views!
Then what is the power of the Soul of souls? (God).
Bread is the food of the body, yet consider,
How can it be the food of the soul, O son?
Flesh-born man by force of soul
Cleaves mountains with tunnels and mines.
The might of Ferhad's soul cleft a hill;
The might of the Soul's soul cleaves the moon; 5
If the heart opens the mouth of mystery's store,
The soul springs up swiftly to highest heaven.
If tongue discourses of hidden mysteries,
It kindles a fire that consumes the world.
Behold, then, God's action and man's action;
Know, action does belong to us ; this is evident.
If no actions proceeded from men,
How could you say, 'Why act ye thus?'
The agency of God is the cause of our action,
Our actions are the signs of God's agency;
Nevertheless our actions are freely willed by us,
Whence our recompense is either hell or 'The Friend.'"

*NOTES:

1. The poet's insistence on the doctrine of God being the Fa'il i
Hakiki, or Only Real Agent, without whose word no being and no
action can be, leads him to the question of freewill and compulsion
of man's will (see Gulshan i Raz, I. 555).

2. So Gulshan i Raz, I. 442.

3. The leading principle of all mysticism is that, independently of
sense and reason, man possesses an inward sense, or intuition,
which conveys to him a knowledge of God by direct apprehension
(see Gulshan i Raz. I. 431).

4. Their wills are identified with God's will, as in the case of the saint

Daquqi (infra, Book III. Story XII.)
5. As a sign of the last day (Koran liv. 1).

STORY VII.

The Merchant and his Clever Parrot.

There was a certain merchant who kept a parrot in a cage. Being about to travel to Hindustan on business, he asked the parrot if he had any message to send to his kinsmen in that country, and the parrot desired him to tell them that he was kept confined in a cage. The merchant promised to deliver this message, and on reaching Hindustan, duly delivered it to the first flock of parrots he saw. On hearing it one of them at once fell down dead. The merchant was annoyed with his own parrot for having sent such a fatal message, and on his return home sharply rebuked his parrot for doing so. But the parrot no sooner heard the merchant's tale than ho too fell down dead in his cage. The merchant, after lamenting his death, took his corpse out of the cage and threw it away; but, to his surprise, the corpse immediately recovered life, and flew away, explaining that the Hindustani parrot had only feigned death to suggest this way of escaping from confinement in a cage.

Saints are preserved from all harm 1.
As to a "man of heart," he takes no hurt,
Even though he should eat deadly poison.
He who gains health from practicing abstinence is safe;
The poor disciple is safe in the midst of fever.
The prophet said, "O disciple, though you be bold,
Yet enter not into conflict with every foe."
Within you is a Nimrod; enter not his fire;
But if you must do so, first become an Abraham. 2
If you are neither swimmer nor seaman,
Cast not yourself into the sea out of self-conceit.
A swimmer brings pearls from the deep sea;
Yea, he plucks gain from the midst of perils.
If the saint handles earth, it becomes gold;
If a sinner handles gold, it turns to dust.
Whereas the saint is well-pleasing to God,
In his actions his hand is the hand of God.
But the sinner's hand is the hand of Satan and demons,
Because he is ensnared in falsity and fraud.
If folly meets him, he takes it for wisdom;

31

Yea, the learning gained by the wicked is folly.
Whatever a sick man eats is a source of sickness,
But if a saint imbibe infidelity it becomes faith.
Ah! footman who contendest with horsemen,
Thou wilt not succeed in carrying the day!
The jealousy of God 3.
The whole world is jealous for this cause,
That God surpasseth the world in jealousy.
God is as a soul and the world as a body,
And bodies derive their good and evil from souls.
He to whom the sanctuary of true prayer is revealed
Deems it shameful to turn back to mere formal religion.
He who is master of the robes of a king
Brings shame on his lord by petty huckstering.
He who is admitted to the king's presence-chamber
Would show disrespect by tarrying at the doorway.
If the king grants him license to kiss his hand,
He would err were he to kiss merely the king's foot.
Though to lay head at the king's feet is due obeisance,
In the case supposed it would be wrong to kiss the feet.
The king's jealousy would be kindled against him
Who, after he had seen his face, preferred his mere perfume.
God's jealousy may be likened to a grain of wheat,
But man's jealousy is but empty chaff.
For know ye that the source of jealousy is in God,
And man's jealousy is only an offshoot from God's.
But, let me now quit this subject, and make complaint
Of the severity of That Fickle Fair One.
Complaints of God's harsh dealings with His adoring slaves.
"Wherefore dost thou abandon thy creed and faith?
What matters it if it be heathen or true?
Why hast thou forsaken thy Beloved?
What matters it if she be fair or ugly?" 4
Let me then, I say, make complaint
Of the severity of That Fickle Fair One.
I cry, and my cries sound sweet in His ear;
He requires from the two worlds cries and groans.
How shall I not wail under His chastening hand?
How shall I not be in the number of those bewitched by Him?

32

How shall I be other than night without His day?
Without the vision of His face that illumes the day?
His bitters are very sweets to my soul,
My sad heart is a lively sacrifice to my Beloved.
I am enamoured of my own grief and pain,
For it makes me well-pleasing to my peerless King.
I use the dust of my grief as salve for my eyes,
That my eyes, like seas, may teem with pearls.
The tears which are shed because of His chastening
Are very pearls, though men deem them mere tears.
'Tis "The Soul of souls" of whom I am making complaint;
Yet I do not complain; I merely state my case.
My heart says, "He has injured me,"
But I laugh at these pretended injuries.
Do me justice, O Thou who art the glory of the just,
Who art the throne, and I the lintel of Thy door!
But, in sober truth, where are throne and doorway?
Where are "We" and "I?" There where our Beloved is!
O Thou, who art exempt from "Us" and "Me,"
Who pervadest the spirits of all men and women;
When man and woman become one, Thou art that One!
When their union is dissolved, lo! Thou abidest!
Thou hast made these "Us" and "Me" for this purpose,
To wit, to play chess with them by Thyself. 5
When Thou shalt become one entity with "Us" and "You."
Then wilt Thou show true affection for these lovers.
When these "We" and "Ye" shall all become one Soul,
Then they will be lost and absorbed in the "Beloved."
These are plain truths. Come then, O Lord!
Who art exalted above description and explanation!
Is it possible for the bodily eye to behold Thee?
Can mind of man conceive Thy frowns and Thy smiles?
Are hearts, when bewitched by Thy smiles and frowns, 6
In a fit state to see the vision of Thyself?
When our hearts are bewitched by Thy smiles and frowns,
Can we gain life from these two alternating states?
The fertile garden of love, as it is boundless,
Contains other fruits besides joy and sorrow.
The true lover is exalted above these two states,

He is fresh and green independently of autumn or spring!
Pay tithe on Thy beauty, O Beauteous One!
Tell forth the tale of the Beloved, every whit!
For through coquetry His glances
Are still inflicting fresh wounds on my heart.
I gave Him leave to shed my blood, if He willed it;
I only said, "Is it right? " and He forsook me.
Why dost Thou flee from the cries of us on earth?
Why pourest Thou sorrow on the heart of the sorrowful?
O Thou who, as each new morn dawns from the east,
Art seen uprising anew, like a bright fountain!
What excuse makest Thou for Thy witcheries?
O Thou whose lips are sweeter than sugar,
Thou that ever renewest the life of this old world,
Hear the cry of this lifeless body and heart!
But, for God's sake, leave off telling of the Rose;
Tell of the Bulbul who is severed from his Rose.
My ardour arises not from joy or grief,
My sense mates not with illusion and fancy.
My condition is different, for it is strange.
Deny it not ! God is all-powerful.
Argue not from the condition of common men,
Stumble not at severity and at mercy.
For mercy and severity, joy and sorrow, are transient,
And transient things die; "God is heir of all." 7
"Tis dawn! O Protector and Asylum of the dawn!
Make excuse for me to my lord Husamu-'d-Din!
Thou makest excuses for c(Universal Reason and Soul; 8
Soul of souls and Gem of life art Thou!
The light of my dawn is a beam from Thy light,
Shining in the morning draught of Thy protection!
Since Thy gift keeps me, as it were, intoxicated,
What is this spiritual wine that causes me this joy?
Natural wine lacks the ferment in my breast,
The spheres lag behind me in revolutions!
Wine is intoxicated with me, not I with it!
The world takes its being from me, not I from it!
I am like bees, and earthly bodies like wax, 9
I build up these bodies as with my own wax!

*NOTES:

1. This is a comment on the saying of Faridu-'d-Din Attar, "Thou art a man of lusts, O fool! In dust eat blood! but if a man of heart eats poison, 'tis as honey."
2. See Koran xxi. 68, and Rodwell's note.
3. This is a comment on the Hadis, "Verily Sa'd is a jealous man, and I am more jealous than he, and God is more jealous than I, and of His jealousy He prohibits 'All pollutions, both outward and inward.'" (Koran vi. 152.)
4. This is a quotation from Hakim Sanai, and forms the text of the following discourse.
5. See Gulshan i Raz, I. 140, and Omar Khayyam Quatr., 270.
6. See Gulshan i Raz, I. 745: Frowns are the occultation of the Beloved by the veil of phenomena; smiles, the revelation of Absolute Being to its votaries. Sa'di (Gulistan, Book II. Story XI.) says: "The vision, of God to the pious consists of manifestation and occultation; He shows Himself, and again withdraws Himself from our sight."
7. Koran xv. 23.
8. i.e., the Logos, and First Soul, upposed to be referred to in the text: "O men, fear your Lord, who hath created you from one Soul, and of him created his wife" (Koran iv. I). See Gulshan i Raz, I. 203.
9. i.e., in his spiritual exaltation he feels himself as the Logos, where from tho whole material creation emanates.

STORY VIII.
The Harper.

In the time of the Khalifa 'Omar there lived a harper, whose voice
was as sweet as that of the angel Israfil, and who was in great
request at all feasts. But he grew old, and his voice broke, and no one
would employ him any longer. In despair he went to the burial-
ground of
Yathrub, and there played his harp to God, looking to Him for
recompense. Having finished his melody he fell asleep, and
dreamed he was in heaven. The same night a divine voice came to
'Omar, directing him to go to the burial-ground, and relieve an old
man whom he should find there. 'Omar proceeded to the place,
found the harper, and gave him money, promising him more when
he should need it. The harper cast away his harp, saying that it had
diverted him from God, and expressed great contrition for his past
sins. 'Omar then instructed him that his worldly journey was now
over, and that he must not give way to contrition for the past, as he
was now entered into the state of ecstasy and intoxication of union
with God, and in this exalted state regard to past and future should
be swept away. The harper acted on his instructions, and sang no
more.
Apology for applying the term "Bride" to God.
Mustafa became beside himself at that sweet call,
His prayer failed on "the night of the early morning halt."
He lifted not head from that blissful sleep," 1
So that his morning prayer was put off till noon.
On that, his wedding night, in presence of his bride,
His pure soul attained to kiss her hands.
Love and mistress are both veiled and hidden,
Impute it not as a fault if I call Him "Bride."
I would have kept silence from fear of my Beloved,
If He had granted me but a moment's respite.
But He said, "Speak on, 'tis no fault,
'Tis naught but the necessary result of the hidden decree,
'Tis a fault only to him who only sees faults.
How can the Pure Hidden Spirit notice faults?"
Faults seem so to ignorant creatures,

Not in the sight of the Lord of Benignity.
Blasphemy even may be wisdom in the Creator's si ht,
Whereas from our point of view it is grievous sin.
If one fault occur among a hundred beauties
'Tis as one dry stick in a garden of green herbs.
Both weigh equally in the scales
For the two resemble body and soul.
Wherefore the sages have said not idly,
" The bodies of the righteous are as pure souls."
Their words, their actions, their praises,
Are all as a pure soul without spot or blemish.
'Omar rebukes the Harper for brooding over
and bewailing the past.
Then 'Omar said to him, "This wailing of thine
Shows thou art still in a state of ' sobriety.'"
Afterwards he thus urged him to quit that state
And called him out of his beggary to absorption in God:
"Sobriety savours of memory of the past;
Past and future are what veil God from our sight.
Burn up both of them with fire! How long
Wilt thou be partitioned by these segments as a reed?
So long as a reed has partitions 'tis not privy to secrets,
Nor is it vocal in response to lip and breathing.
While circumambulating the house thou art a stranger;
When thou enterest in thou art at home.
Thou whose knowledge is ignorance of the Giver of knowledge,
Thy wailing contrition is worse than thy sin.
The road of the 'annihilated' is another road;
Sobriety is wrong, and a straying from that other road.
O thou who seekest to be contrite for the past,
How wilt thou be contrite for this contrition?
At one time thou adorest the music of the lute,
At another embracest wailing and weeping."
While the "Discerner" reflected these mysteries,
The heart of the harper was emancipated.
Like a soul he was freed from weeping and rejoicing,
His old life died, and he was regenerated.
Amazement fell upon him at that moment,
For he was exalted above earth and heaven,

An uplifting of the heart surpassing all uplifting;
I cannot describe it ; if you can, say on!
Ecstasy and words beyond all ecstatic words;
Immersion in the glory of the Lord of glory!
Immersion wherefrom was no extrication,
As it were identification with the Very Ocean!
Partial Reason is as naught to Universal Reason,
If one impulse dependent on another impulse be naught;
But when that impulse moves this impulse,
The waves of that sea rise to this point; 2

*NOTES:
1. The night of his marriage with Safiyya.
2. i.e., he is possessed by the Deity as an "Energumen," and the Deity works these ecstatic states in him.

STORY IX.

The Arab and his Wife.
An Arab lived with his wife in the desert in extreme poverty, so that
they became a reproach to their neighbours. The wife at last lost
patience, and began to abuse her husband, and to urge him to
improve their condition. The Arab rebuked her for her covetousness,
reminding her that the Prophet had said, "Poverty is my glory," and
showing her how poverty was a better preparation for death than
riches, and finally threatening to divorce her if she persisted in her
querulous ways. The wife, however, by blandishments reduced her
husband to obedience, as wives always do, and made him promise
to carry out her wishes. She directed him to go and represent their
case to the Khalifa at Bagdad, and to make him an offering of a pot
of water, that being the only present they could afford to make.
Accordingly the Arab travelled to Bagdad, and laid his offering at
the feet of the Khalifa, who received it graciously, and in return filled
the pot with pieces of gold, and then sent him back to his home in a
boat up the river Tigris. The Arab was lost in wonder at the
benignity of the Khalifa, who had recompensed him so bountifully
for his petty offering of a drop of water. The story contains several
digressions, on Pharaoh, on the prophet Salih, and on Adam and the
angels, and the poet, apropos of its disconnectedness, compares it to
eternity, as it has no beginning and no end.
Men subdued by women's wiles.
In this manner she pleaded with gentle coaxing,
The while her tears fell upon her cheeks.
How could his firmness and endurance abide
When even without tears she could charm his heart?
That rain brought forth a flash of lightning
Which kindled a spark in the heart of that poor man.
Since the man was the slave of her fair face,
How was it when she stooped to slavish entreaties?
When she whose airs set thy heart a-quaking,
When she weeps, how feelest thou then?
When she whose coquetry makes thy heart bleed
Condescends to entreaties, how is it then?

She who subdues us with her pride and severity,
What plea is left us when she begins to plead?
When she who traded in naught but bloodshed
Submits at last, ah! what a profit she makes!
God has adorned them "fair in the sight of men;" 1
From her whom God has adorned how can man escape?
Since He created him "to dwell together with her," 2
How can Adam sever himself from his Eve?
Though he be Rustum, son of Zal, and braver than Hamza,
Yet he is submissive to the behests of his dame.
He by whose preaching the world was entranced
Was he who spake the two words, "O Humaira!" 3
Though water prevails over fire in might,
Yet it boils by fire when in a cauldron.
When the cauldron intervenes between these two,
Air (desire) makes as naught the action of the water.
Apparently thou art the ruler of thy wife, like water;
In reality thou art ruled by and suppliant to her.
Such is the peculiarity of man,
He cannot withstand animal desire; that is his failing.
The Prophet said that women hold dominion
Over sages and over men of heart,
But that fools, again, hold the upper hand over women,
Because fools are violent and exceedingly froward.
They have no tenderness or gentleness or amity,
Because the animal nature sways their temperament.
Love and tenderness are qualities of humanity,
Passion and lust are qualities of animality.
Woman is a ray of God, not a mere mistress,
The Creator's self, as it were, not a mere creature!
Moses and Pharaoh, alike doers of God's will,
as Light and Darkness. Poison and Antidote.
Verily, both Moses and Pharaoh walked in the right way,
Though seemingly the one did so, and the other not.
By day Moses wept before God,
At midnight Pharaoh lifted up his cry,
Saying, "What a yoke is this upon my neck, O God!
Were it not for this yoke who would boast, 'I am ?'
Because Thou hast made Moses' face bright as the moon,

And hast made the moon of my face black in the face.
Can my star ever shine brighter than the moon?
If it be eclipsed, what remedy have I?
Though princes and kings beat drums,
And men beat cymbals because of my eclipse, 4
They beat their brass dishes and raise a clamour,
And make my moon ashamed thereby,
I, who am Pharaoh, woe is me! The people's clamour
Confounds my boast, 'I am Lord Supreme!' 5
Moses and I are Thy nurslings both alike,
Yet Thy axe cuts down tho branches in Thy woods.
Some of these branches Thou plantest in the ground,
Others Thou castest away as useless.
Can branch strive against axe? Not so.
Can branch elude the power of the axe? Nay,
O Lord of the power that dwells in Thy axe,
In mercy make these crooked things straight!"
Man and wife types of the spirit and the flesh.
The dissension of this husband and wife is a parable;
They are types of thy animal and rational souls.
This husband and wife are the reason and the flesh,
A couple joined together for good and for evil.
And in this earthly house this linked pair
Day and night are ever at variance and strife.
The wife is ever seeking dainties for domestic needs,
Namely, bread and meat and her own dignity and position.
Like the wife, the animal soul seeks comfort,
Sometimes carnal, sometimes ambitious;
Reason has no care for these matters,
In its mind is naught but regard to Allah.
Though the secret moral hereof is a bait and snare,
Hear its outward form to the end.
If spiritual manifestations had been sufficient,
The creation of the world had been needless and vain.
If spiritual thought were equivalent to love of God,
Outward forms of temples and prayers would not exist.
Presents which friends make one to another
Are naught but signs and indications,
To give outward testimony and witness

Of the love concealed within the heart.
Because outward attentions are evidence
Of secret love, O beloved!
The witness may be true or false,
Now drunk with real wine, now with sour whey;
He who drinks fermented whey displays drunkenness,
Makes a noise, and reels to and fro.
That hypocrite in prayers and fasts
Displays exceeding diligence,
That men may think him drunk with love of God;
But if you look into the truth, he is drowned in hypocrisy.
In fine, outward actions are guides
To show the way to what is concealed within.
Sometimes the guide is true, sometimes false,
Sometimes a help, and at other times a hindrance.
O Lord, grant, in answer to my prayers, discernment,
That I may know such false signs from the true!
Know you how discernment accrues to the sense?
'Tis when sense "sees by the light of Allah."
If effects are obscure, still causes testify;
Kindred, for instance, shows that there is love.
But he to whom God's light is the guide
Is no longer a slave to effects and causes.
When the light of Allah illumes his senses,
A man is no longer a slave to effects.
When love of God kindles a flame in the inward man,
He burns, and is freed from effects.
He has no need of signs to assure him of love,
For love casts its own light up to heaven.
Other details are wanting to complete this subject,
But take this much, and all hail to you!
Though reality is exposed to view in this form,
Form is at once nigh to and far from reality.
For instance, these two resemble water and a tree;
When you look to their essence they are far apart;
Yet see how quickly a seed becomes a high tree
Out of water, along with earth and sunshine!
If you turn your eyes to their real essence,
These two are far, far apart from each other!

But let us quit this talk of essences and properties,
And return to the story of those two wealth-seekers.
How God made Adam superior to the Angels
in wisdom and honour.
He said, "By Allah, who knoweth hidden secrets,
Who created pure Adam out of dust;
In the form, three cubits high, which he gave him,
He displayed the contents of all spirits, all decrees!
Communicated to him the indelible tablet of existence, 6
That he might know all that is written on those tablets,
A11 that should be first and last to endless eternity
He taught him, with the knowledge of his own 'names,' 7
So that the angels were beside themselves at his instruction,
And gained more sanctity from his sanctification.
The expansion of their minds, which Adam brought about,
Was a thing unequalled by the expansion of the heavens.
For the wide expanse of that pure mind
The wide space of the seven heavens was not enough."
The Prophet said that God has declared,
"I am not contained in aught above or below,
I am not contained in earth or sky, or even
In highest heaven. Know this for a surety. O beloved!
Yet am I contained in the believer's heart!
If ye seek me, search in such hearts!"
He said also, "Enter the hearts of my servants 8
To gain the paradise of beholding Me, O fearer of God."
Highest heaven, with all its light and wide expanse,
When it beheld Adam, was shaken from its place!
Highest heaven is greatness itself revealed;
But what is form when reality draws nigh?
Every angel declared, "In times of yore
We bore friendship to the plains of earth;
We were wont to sow the seed of service on the earth,
Wherefore we bore a wondrous attachment to it.
What was this attachment to that house of earth
When our own natures are heavenly?
What was the friendship of lights like us to darkness?
How can light dwell together with darkness?
O Adam! that friendship arose from the scent of thee,

Because the earth is the warp and weft of thy body.
Thy earthly body was taken from there,
Thy pure spirit of light was shed down from here!
But our souls were enlightened by thy spirit 9
Long, long before earth had diverted it to itself.
We used to be on earth, ignorant of tho earth,
Ignorant of the treasure buried within it.
When we were commanded to depart from that place,
We felt sorrow at turning our steps away from it.
So that we raised many questions, saying,
' O Lord! who will come to take our place?
Wilt Thou barter the glory of our praises and homage
For the vain babble (of men)?'
The commands of God then diffused joy upon us; He said,
'What are ye saying at such length?
What ye give tongue to so foolishly
Is as the words of spoiled children to their father.
I knew of myself what ye thought,
But I desired that ye should speak it;
As this boasting of yours is very improper,
So shall my mercy be shown to prevail over my wrath:
O angels, in order to show forth that prevailing,
I inspired that pretension to cavil and doubt;
If you say your say, and I forbear to punish you,
The gainsayers of my mercy must hold their peace.
My mercy equals that of a hundred fathers and mothers;
Every soul that is born is amazed thereat.
Their mercy is as the foam of the sea of my mercy;
It is mere foam of waves, but the sea abides ever!
What more shall I say? In that earthly shell
There is naught but foam of foam of foam of foam!'"
God is that foam; God is also that pure sea,
For His words are neither a temptation nor a vain boast.
Plurality and Partial Evil, though seemingly
opposed to Unity, subserve Good.
The story is now concluded, with its ups and downs,
Like lovers' musings, without beginning or ending.
It has no beginning, even as eternity,
Nor ending, for 'tis akin to world without end.

Or like water, each drop whereof is at once
Beginning and end, and also has no beginning or end.
But God forbid! This story is not a vain fable,
'Tis the ready money of your state and mine, be sure!
Before every Sufi who is enlightened
Whatever is past is never mentioned.
When his whole thoughts are absorbed in present ecstasy,
No thought of consequences enters his mind. 10
Arab, water-pot, and angels are all ourselves!
"Whatsoever turneth from God is turned from Him." 11
Know the husband is reason, the wife lust and greed;
She is vested with darkness and a gainsayer of reason.
Learn now whence springs the root of this circumstance,
From this, that the Whole has parts of divers kinds.
These parts of the Whole are not parts in relation to it,
Not in the way that rose's scent is a part of the rose.
The beauty of the green shoot is part of the rose's beauty,
But the turtle-dove's cooing is a part of that Bulbuls music.
But if I engage in doubts and answers,
How can I give water to thirsty souls?
Yet, if you are perplexed by Whole and finite parts,
Have patience, for c(patience is the key of joy."
Be abstinent, abstinent from vague thoughts,
Since there are lions in that desert (of thoughts).
Abstinence is the prince of medicines,
As scratching only aggravates a scab.
Abstinence is certainly the root of medicine;
Practise abstinence, see how it invigorates thy soul!
Accept this counsel and give ear thereto,
That it may be to thee as an earring of gold!
Nay, not a mere earring, but that thou mayest be a mine of gold,
Or that thou mayest surpass moon and Pleiades.
First, know creation is in various forms;
Souls are as various as the letters from Alif to Ya.
In this variety of letters there seems disorder,
Though in fact they agree in an integral unity.
In one aspect they are opposed, in another united;
In one aspect capricious, in another serious.
The day of judgment is the day of tho great review;

Whoso is fair and enlightened longs for that review;
Whoso, like a Hindoo, is black (with sin),
The day of review will sound the knell of his disgrace.
Since he has not a face like a sun,
He desires only night like to a veil!
If his thorn puts not forth a single rosebud,
The spring in disclosing him is his foe.
But he who is from head to foot a perfect rose or lily,
To him spring brings rejoicing.
The useless thorn desires the autumn,
That autumn may associate itself with the garden;
And hide the rose's beauty and the thorn's shame,
That men may not see the bloom of the one and the other's shame,
That common stone and pure ruby may appear all as one.
True, the Gardener knows the difference even in autumn,
But the sight of One is better than the world's sight.
That One Person is Himself the world, as He is the sun,
And every star in heaven is a part of the sun.
That One Person is Himself the world, and the rest
Are all His dependents and parasites, O man!
He is the perfect world, yet He is single;
He holds in hand the writing of the whole of existence.
Wherefore all forms and colours of beauty cry out,
" Good news! good news! Lo! the spring is at hand!"
If the blossoms did not shine as bright helmets,
How could the fruits display their globes?
When the blossoms are shed the fruits come to a head,
When tho body is destroyed the soul lifts up its head.
The fruit is the substance, the blossom only its form,
Blossom the good news, and fruit the promised boon.
When the blossoms fall the fruit appears,
When the former vanish the fruit is tasted.
Till bread is broken, how can it serve as food?
Till the grapes are crushed, how can they yield wine?
Till citrons be pounded up with drugs,
How can they afford healing to the sick?

*NOTES:

1. Koran iii. 12.
2. Koran iii. 189.
3. Muhammad said these words to his wife, Ayisha.
4. Compare the ancient custom of ringing bells to still thunder.
5. Koran lxxix. 24. Pharaoh's boast.
6. The tablet on which God writes His eternal decrees.
7. Koran ii. 29.
8. Koran lxxxix. 29.
9. The Logos, the first of created beings, was afterwards embodied in Adam, the "Perfect Man," or Microcosm.
10. He is the "son of the time present and instant," as said above.
11. Koran li. 9.

STORY X.

The Man who was Tattooed.
It was the custom of the men of Qazwin to have various devices
tattooed upon their bodies. A certain coward went to the artist to
have such a device tattooed on his back, and desired that it might be
the figure of a lion. But when he felt the pricks of the needles he
roared with pain, and said to the artist, "What part of the lion are
you now painting?" The artist replied, "I am doing the tail." The
patient cried, "Never mind the tail; go on with another part." The
artist accordingly began in another part, but the patient again cried
out and told him to try somewhere else. Wherever the artist applied
his needles, the patient raised similar objections, till at last the artist
dashed all his needles and pigments on the ground, and refused to
proceed any further.
The Prophet's counsels to 'Ali to follow the direction of the Pir or
Spiritual Guide, and to endure his chastisements patiently.
The Prophet said to 'Ali, "O 'Ali,
Thou art the Lion of God, a hero most valiant;
Yet confide not in thy lion-like valour,
But seek refuge under the palm-trees of the 'Truth.'
Whoso takes obedience as his exemplar
Shares its proximity to the ineffable Presence.
Do thou seek to draw near to Reason; let not thy heart
Rely, like others, on thy own virtue and piety.
Come under the shadow of the Man of Reason, l
Thou canst not find it in the road of the traditionists.
That man enjoys close proximity to Allah;
Turn not away from obedience to him in any wise;
For he makes the thorn a bed of roses,
And gives sight to the eyes of the blind.
His shadow on earth is as that of Mount Qaf,
His spirit is as a Simurgh soaring on high.
He lends aid to the slaves of the friends of God,
And advances to high place them who seek him.
Were I to tell his praises till the last day,
My words would not be too many nor admit of curtailment,
He is the sun of the spirit, not that of the sky,

For from his light men and angels draw life.
That sun is hidden in the form of a man,
Understand me! Allah knows the truth.
O 'Ali, out of all forms of religious service
Choose thou the shadow of that dear friend of God!
Every man takes refuge in some form of service,
And chooses for himself some asylum;
Do thou seek refuge in the shadow of the wise man,
That thou mayest escape thy fierce secret foes.
Of all forms of service this is fittest for thee;
Thou shalt surpass all who were before thee.
Having chosen thy Director, be submissive to him,
Even as Moses submitted to the commands of Khizr; 2
Have patience with Khizr's actions, O sincere one!
Lest he say, 'There is a partition between us.'
Though he stave in thy boat, yet hold thy peace;
Though he slay a young man, heave not a sigh.
God declares his hand to be even as God's hand,
For He saith, (The hand of God is over their hands.' 3
The hand of God impels him and gives him life;
Nay, not life only, but an eternal soul.
A friend is needed; travel not the road alone,
Take not thy own way through this desert!
Whoso travels this road alone
Only does so by aid of the might of holy men.
The hand of the Director is not weaker than theirs;
His hand is none other than the grasp of Allah!
If absent saints can confer such protection,
Doubtless present saints are more powerful than absent.
If such food be bestowed on the absent,
What dainties may not the guest who is present expect?
The courtier who attends in the presence of the king
Is served better than the stranger outside the gate.
The difference between them is beyond calculation;
One sees the light, the other only the veil.
Strive to obtain entrance within,
If thou wouldst not remain as a ring outside the door.
Having chosen thy Director, be not weak of heart,
Nor yet sluggish and lax as water and mud;

But if thou takest umbrage at every rub,
How wilt thou become a polished mirror?"
*NOTES:
1. i.e., the Pir, or Perfect Shaikh, or Spiritual Director. So St. John of
the Cross and St. Theresa enjoin obedience to the Director (Vaughan,
xii. 122).
2. See Koran xviii. 77 for the story of Moses and Khizr. It is also given
in Parnell's 'Hermit.'
3. Koran xlviii. 10.

STORY XI.

The Lion who Hunted with the Wolf and the Fox.
A lion took a wolf and a fox with him on a hunting excursion, and
succeeded in catching a wild ox, an ibex, and a hare. He then
directed the wolf to divide the prey. The wolf proposed to award the
ox to the lion, the ibex to himself, and the hare to the fox. The lion
was enraged with the wolf because he had presumed to talk of "I"
and "Thou," and "My share" and "Thy share" when it all belonged of
right to the lion, and he slew the wolf with one blow of his paw.
Then, turning to the fox, he ordered him to make the division. The
fox, rendered wary by the fate of the wolf, replied that the whole
should be the portion of the lion. The lion, pleased with his self-
abnegation, gave it all up to him, saying, "Thou art no longer a fox,
but myself."
Till man destroys "self" he is no true friend of God.
Once a man came and knocked at the door of his friend.
His friend said, "who art thou. O faithful one?"
He said, "'Tis I." He answered, "There is no admittance.
There is no room for the 'raw' at my well-cooked feast.
Naught but fire of separation and absence
Can cook the raw one and free him from hypocrisy!
Since thy 'self' has not yet left thee,
Thou must be burned in fiery flames."
The poor man went away, and for one whole year
Journeyed burning with grief for his friend's absence.
His heart burned till it was cooked; then he went again
And drew near to the house of his friend.
He knocked at the door in fear and trepidation
Lest some careless word might fall from his lips.
His friend shouted, "Who is that at the door?"
He answered, "'Tis Thou who art at the door. O Beloved!"
The friend said, "Since 'tis I, let me come in,
There is not room for two 'I's' in one house."

STORY XII.
Joseph a,Žd the Mirror.

An old friend came to pay his respects to Joseph, and, after some
remarks upon the bad behaviour of his brethren, Joseph asked him
what present he had brought to show his respect. The friend replied
that he had long considered what gift would be most suitable to
offer, and at last had fixed upon a mirror, which he accordingly
produced from his pocket and presented to Joseph, at the same time
begging him to admire his own beauteous face in it.
Defect and Not-being the Mirror wherein
Absolute Perfect Being is reflected 1.
He drew forth a mirror from his side
A mirror is what Beauty busies itself with.
Since Not-being is tho mirror of Being,
If you are wise, choose Not-being (self-abnegation).
Being may be displayed in that Not-being,
Wealthy men show their liberality on the poor.
He who is an hungered is the clear mirror of bread,
The tinder is the mirror of the flint and steel.
Not-being and Defect, wherever they occur,
Are the mirrors of the Beauty of all beings.
Because Not-being is a clear filtered essence,
Wherein all these beings are infused.
When a garment is made by a good tailor,
'Tis an evidence of the tailor's art.
Logs of wood would not be duly shaped
Did not the carpenter plan outline and detail.
The leech skilled in setting bones goes
Where lies the patient with a broken leg.
If there were no sick and infirm,
How could the excellence of the leech's art be seen?
If vile base copper were not mingled,
How could the alchemist show his skill?
Defects are the mirrors of the attributes of Beauty,

The base is the mirror of the High and Glorious One,
Because one contrary shows forth its contrary, 2
As honey's sweetness is shown by vinegar's sourness.
Whoso recognizes and confesses his own defects
Is hastening in the way that leads to perfection!
But he advances not towards the Almighty
Who fancies himself to be perfect.
No sickness worse than fancying thyself perfect
Can infect thy soul, O arrogant misguided one!
Shed many tears of blood from eyes and heart,
That this self-satisfaction may be driven out.
The fault of Iblis lay in saying, "I am better than he," 3
And this same weakness lurks in the soul of all creatures.
*NOTES:
1. Compare the parallel passage in Gulshan i Raz, 1. 135, and the notes thereon.
2. Cp. "Religio Medici," Sect. 35: "Herein is divinity conformant unto philosophy, and not only generation founded on contrarieties, but also creation. God, being all things, is contrary unto nothing; out of which were made all things, and so nothing became something, and Omneity informed nullity into existence."
3. Koran vii. II.

STORY XIII.
The Prophet's Scribe.

The Prophet had a scribe who used to write down the texts that fell
from his lips. At last this scribe became so conceited that he
imagined all this heavenly wisdom proceeded from his own wit,
and not from the Prophet. Puffed up with self-importance, he
fancied himself inspired, and his heart was hardened against his
master, and he became a renegade, like the fallen angels Harut and
Marut. He took his own foolish surmises to be the truth, whereas
they were all wide of the mark, as those of the deaf man who went
to condole with a sick neighbour and answered all his remarks at
cross purposes.
How philosophers deceive themselves.
On the last day, 1 "when Earth shall quake with quaking,"
This earth shall give witness of her condition.
For she "shall tell out her tidings openly,"
Yea, earth and her rocks shall tell them forth!
The philosopher reasons from base analogies
(True reason comes not out of a dark corner) ;
The philosopher (I say) denies this in his pride of intellect.
Say to him, "Go, dash thy head against a wall!"
The speech of water, of earth, of mire,
Is audible by the ears of men of heart!
Tho philosopher, who denies Divine Providence,
Is a stranger to the perceptions of saints.
He says that the flashes of men's morbid imaginations
Instil many vain fancies into men's minds.
But, on the contrary, 'tis his perverseness and want of faith
Which implant in himself this vain fancy of negation.
The philosopher denies the existence of the Devil;
At the same time he is the Devil's laughing-stock.
If thou hast not seen the Devil, look at thyself,
Without demon's aid how came that blue turban 2 on thy brow?
Whosoever has a doubt or disquietude in his heart

Is a secret denier and philosopher.
Now and then he displays firm belief,
But that slight dash of philosophy blackens his face.
Beware, O believers! That lurks in you too;
You may develop innumerable states of mind.
All the seventy and two heresies lurk in you;
Have a care lest one day they prevail over you!
He in whose breast the leaf of true faith is grown
Must tremble as a leaf from fear of such a catastrophe.
Thou makest a mock of Iblis and the Devil,
Because thou art a fine man in thy own sight;
But when thy soul shall tell thy wretched faults,
What lamentation thou wilt cause to the faithful!
The sellers of base gold sit smiling in their shops,
Because the touchstone is not as yet in their sight.
O Veiler of sins! strip not the veil from us;
Lend us aid on the day of trial!
*NOTES:
1. Koran xcix. 1-4.
2. Blue turbans were considered a sign of hypocrisy (Hafiz, Ode 5).

STORY XIV.
The Chinese and the Greek Artists.

The Chinese and the Greeks disputed before the Sultan which of
them were the better painters; and, in order to settle the dispute, the
Sultan allotted to each a house to be painted by them. The Chinese
procured all kinds of paints, and coloured their house in the most
elaborate way. The Greeks, on the other hand, used no colours at all,
but contented themselves with cleansing the walls of their house
from all filth, and burnishing them till they were as clear and bright
as the heavens. When the two houses were offered to tho Sultan's
inspection, that painted by tho Chinese was much admired; but the
Greek house carried off the palm, as all the colours of the other
house were reflected on its walls with an endless variety of shades
and hues.

Knowledge of the heart preferable
to the knowledge of the schools.
The knowledge of men of heart bears them up,
The knowledge of men of the body weighs them down.
When 'tis knowledge of the heart, it is a friend;
When knowledge of the body, it is a burden.
God saith, "As an ass bearing a load of books," 1
The knowledge which is not of Him is a burden.
Knowledge which comes not immediately from Him
Endures no longer than the rouge of the tirewoman.
Nevertheless, if you bear this burden in a right spirit
'Twill be removed, and you will obtain joy.
See you bear not that burden out of vainglory,
Then you will behold a store of true knowledge within.
When you mount the steed of this true knowledge,
Straightway the burden will fall from your back.
If you drink not His cup, how will you escape lusts?
You, who seek no more of Him than to name His name?
What do His name and fame suggest? The idea of Him.
And the idea of Him guides you to union with Him.

Know you a guide without something to which it guides?
Were there no roads there would be no ghouls.
Know you a name without a thing answering to it?
Have you ever plucked a rose (Gul) from Gaf and Lam?
You name His name; go, seek the reality named by it!
Look for the moon in heaven, not in the water!
If you desire to rise above mere names and letters,
Make yourself free from self at one stroke!
Like a sword be without trace of soft iron;
Like a steel mirror, scour off all rust with contrition;
Make yourself pure from all attributes of self,
That you may see your own pure bright essence!
Yea, see in your heart the knowledge of the Prophet,
Without book, without tutor, without preceptor.
The Prophet saith, "He is one of my people,
Whoso is of like temper and spirit with me.
His soul beholds me by the selfsame light
Whereby I myself behold him,
Without traditions and scriptures and histories,
In the fount of the water of life."
Learn the mystery, "I was last night a Kurd,
And this morning am become an Arab." 2
This mystery of "last night" and "this morning"
Leads you into the road that brings you to God.
But if you want an instance of this secret knowledge,
Hear the story of the Greeks and the Chinese.
*NOTES:
1. Koran lxii. 5.
2. Syad Abu'l Wafa, an unlettered Kurd, found a paper with the
words Bismillah upon it, and, after spending the night in prayer,
found himself able to understand Arabic (Luck-now Commentator).

STORY XV.

Counsels of Reserve given by the Prophet to his Freedman Zaid.
At dawn the Prophet said to Zaid,
"How is it with thee this morning, O pure disciple?"
He replied, "Thy faithful slave am I." Again he said,
"If the garden of faith has bloomed, show a token of it."
He answered, "I was athirst many days,
By night I slept not for the burning pangs of love;
So that I passed by days and nights,
As the point of a spear glances off a shield.
For in that state all faith is one,
A hundred thousand years and a moment are all one;
World without beginning and world without end are one;
Reason finds no entrance when mind is thus lost."
The Prophet again urged Zaid to deliver to him a present from that
celestial region, as a token that he had really been there in the spirit.
Zaid answered that he had seen the eight heavens and the seven
hells, and the destinies of all men, whether bound to heaven or hell.
The body, he said, is as a mother, and the soul as her infant, and
death is the time of parturition, when it becomes manifest to what
class the infant soul belongs. As, on the day of judgment it will be
manifest to all men whether a soul belongs to the saved or to the lost,
so now it was plain and manifest to him. He went on to ask the
Prophet if he should publish this secret knowledge of his to all men,
or hold his peace. The Prophet told him to hold his peace. Zaid,
however, proceeded to detail the vision of the last judgment, which
he had seen when in the spirit; and the Prophet again commanded
him to pause, adding that" God is never ashamed to say the truth," I
and allows His Prophet to speak forth the truth, but that for Zaid to
blab forth the secrets seen in ecstatic vision would be wrong. Zaid
replied that it was impossible for one who had once beheld the Sun
of "The Truth" to keep his vision a secret. But the Prophet in reply
instructed him that all men are masters of their own wills, and that
he must not reveal what God has determined to keep secret till the

last day, in order to leave men till then under the stimulus of hope
and fear, and to give them the credit of "believing what is not seen."
2 More honour is given to the warder of a castle who faithfully
executes his trust at a distance from the court than to those courtiers
who serve constantly under the king's own eye. Zaid submitted to
tho Prophet's injunctions, and remained self-contained in his ecstatic
visions. Anecdotes of the sage Luqman, of King Solomon, and of a
conflagration in the days of the Khalifa 'Omar complete the section.
The Prophet's final counsels of "Reserve".
The Prophet said, "My companions are as the stars,
Lights to them that walk aright, missiles against Satan.
If every man had strength of eyesight
To look straight at the light of the sun in heaven,
What need were there of stars, O humble one,
To one who was guided by the light of the sun?
Neither moon nor planets would be needed
By one who saw directly the Sun of 'The Truth.'
The Moon 3 declares, as also the clouds and shadows,
' I am a man, yet it hath been revealed to me.' 4
Like you, I was naturally dark,
'Twas the Sun's revelation that gave me such light.
I still am dark compared to the Sun,
Though I am light compared to the dark souls of men.
Therefore is my light weak, that you may bear it,
For you are not strong enough to bear the dazzling Sun.
I have, as it were, mixed honey with vinegar,
To succour the sickness of your hearts.
When you are cured of your sickness, O invalid,
Then leave out the vinegar and eat pure honey.
When the heart is garnished and swept clear of lust,
Therein 'The God of Mercy sitteth on His throne.' 5
Then God rules the heart immediately,
When it has gained this immediate connection with Him.
This subject is endless; but where is Zaid,
That I may tell him again not to seek notoriety?
'Tis not wise to publish these mysteries,
Since the last day is approaching to reveal all things."
Now you will not find Zaid, for he is fled,
He sprang from the place where the shoes were left, 6

Scattering the shoes in his hurry.
If you had been Zaid, you too would have been lost,
As a star is lost when tho sun shines on it;
For then you see no trace or sign of it,
No place or track of it in tho milky way.
Our senses and our endless discourses
Are annihilated in the light of the knowledge of our King.
Our senses and our reason within us
Are as waves on waves "assembled before us." 7
When night returns and 'tis the time of the sky's levee,
The stars that were hidden come forth to their work.
The people of the world lie unconscious,
With veils drawn over their faces, and asleep;
But when the morn shall burst forth and the sun arise
Every creature will raise its head from its couch;
To the unconscious God will restore consciousness;
They will stand in rings as slaves with rings in ears;
Dancing and clapping hands with songs of praise,
Singing with joy, "Our Lord hath restored us to life!"
Shedding their old skins and bones,
As horsemen stirring up a cloud of dust.
All pressing on from Not-being to Being,
On the last day, as well the thankful as the unthankful.
*NOTES:
1. Koran xxxiii. 53.
2. Koran ii. 2.
3. i.e., the Prophet.
4. Koran xviii. 110.
5. Koran xx. 4.
6. i.e., the vestibule of the house.
7. Koran xxxvi. 53.

STORY XVI.

'Ali's Forbearance.

'Ali, the "Lion of God," was once engaged in conflict with a Magian chief, and in the midst of the struggle the Magian spat in his face. 'Ali, instead of taking vengeance on him, at once dropped his sword, to the Magian's great astonishment. On his inquiring the reason of such forbearance, 'Ali informed him that the "Lion of God" did not destroy life for the satisfaction of his own vengeance, but simply to carry out God's will, and that whenever he saw just cause, he held his hand even in the midst of the strife, and spared the foe. The Prophet, 'Ali continued, had long since informed him that he would die by the hand of his own stirrup-bearer (Ibn Maljun), and the stirrup-bearer had frequently implored 'Ali to kill him, and thus save him from the commission of that great crime; but 'Ali said he always refused to do so, as to him death was as sweet as life, and he felt no anger against his destined assassin, who was only the instrument of God's eternal purpose. The Magian chief, on hearing 'Ali's discourse, was so much affected that he embraced Islam, together with all his family, to the number of fifty souls.

How the Prophet whispered to 'Ali's stirrup-bearer
that he would one day assassinate his master.

"The Prophet whispered in the ear of my servant
That one day he would sever my head from my neck.
The Prophet also warned by inspiration me, his friend,
That the hand of my servant would destroy me.
My servant cried, "O kill me first,
That I may not become guilty of so grievous a sin!"
I replied, "Since my death is to come from thee,
How can I balk the fateful decree?"
He fell at my feet and cried, "O gracious lord,
For God's sake cleave now my body in twain,
That such an evil deed may not be wrought by me,
And my soul burn with anguish for its beloved."
I replied, "What God's pen has written, it has written;
In presence of its writings knowledge is confounded;
There is no anger in my soul against thee,

Because I attribute not this deed to thee;
Thou art God's instrument. God's hand is the agent.
How can I chide or fret at God's instrument?"
He said, "If this be so, why is there retaliation?" 1
I answered, "'Tis from God, and 'tis God's secret;
If He shows displeasure at His own acts,
From His displeasure He evolves a Paradise;
He feels displeasure at His own acts,
Because He is a God of vengeance as of mercy.
In this city of events He is the Lord,
In this realm He is the King who plans all events.
If He crushes His own instruments,
He makes those crushed ones fair in His sight.
Know the great mystery of 'whatever verses we cancel,
Or cause you to forget, we substitute better for them.' 2
Whatever law God cancels, He makes as a weed,
And in its stead He brings forth a rose.
So night cancels the business of the daytime,
When the reason that lights our minds becomes inanimate.
Again, night is cancelled by the light of day,
And inanimate reason is rekindled to life by its rays.
Though darkness produces this sleep and quiet,
Is not the 'water of life' in the darkness? 3
Are not spirits refreshed in that very darkness?
Is not that silence the season of heavenly voices?
For from contraries contraries are brought forth,
Out of darkness was created light.
The Prophet's wars brought about the present peace,
The peace of these latter days resulted from those wars.
That conqueror of hearts cut off a thousand heads,
That the heads of his people might rest in peace."
God's rebuke to Adam for scorning Iblis.
To whomsoever God's order comes,
He must smite with his sword even his own child.
Fear then, and revile not the wicked,
For the wicked are impotent under God's commands.
In presence of God's commands bow down the neck of pride.
Scoff not nor chide even them that go astray!
One day Adam cast a look of contempt and scorn

Upon Iblis, thinking what a wretch he was.
He felt self-important and proud of himself,
And he smiled at the actions of cursed Iblis.
God Almighty cried out to him, "O pure one,
Thou art wholly ignorant of hidden mysteries.
If I were to blab the faults of the unfortunate,
I should root up the mountains from their bases,
And lay bare the secrets of a hundred Adams,
And convert a hundred fresh Iblises into Mosalmans."
Adam answered, "I repent me of my scornful looks;
Such arrogant thoughts shall not be mine again.
O Lord, pardon this rashness in Thy slave;
I repent; chastise me not for these words!"
O Aider of aid-seekers, guide us,
For there is no security in knowledge or wealth;
"Lead not our hearts astray after Thou hast guided us," 4
And avert the evil that the "Pen" has written.
Turn aside from our souls the evil written in our fates,
Repel us not from the tables of purity!
O God, Thy grace is the proper object of our desire;
To couple others with Thee is not proper.
Nothing is bitterer than severance from Thee,
Without Thy shelter there is naught but perplexity.
Our worldly goods rob us of our heavenly goods,
Our body rends the garment of our soul.
Our hands, as it were, prey on our feet;
Without reliance on Thee how can we live?
And if the soul escapes these great perils,
It is made captive as a victim of misfortunes and fears,
Inasmuch as when the soul lacks union with the Beloved,
It abides forever blind and darkened by itself.
If Thou showest not the way, our life is lost;
A life living without Thee esteem as dead!
If Thou findest fault with Thy slaves,
Verily it is right in Thee, O Blessed One!
If Thou shouldst call sun and moon obscure,
If Thou shouldst call the straight cypress crooked,
If Thou shouldst declare the highest heaven base,
Or rich mines and oceans paupers,

All this is the truth in relation to Thy perfection!
Thine is the dominion and the glory and the wealth!
For Thou art exempt from defect and not-being,
Thou givest existence to things non-existent, and again
Thou makest them non-existent.
*NOTES:
1. i,e., why is the rule "an eye for an eye" enjoined in the Koran, ii. 173?
2. Koran ii, 100.
3. Alluding to the "water of life" in the land of darkness discovered by Khizr.
4. Koran iii. 6.

Epilogue to Book I.
Alas! the forbidden fruits were eaten,
And thereby the warm life of reason was congealed.
A grain of wheat eclipsed the sun Of Adam, 1
Like as the Dragon's tail 2 dulls the brightness of the moon.
Behold how delicate is the heart, that a morsel of dust
Clouded its moon with foul obscurity!
When bread is "substance," to eat it nourishes us;
When 'tis empty "form," it profits nothing.
Like as the green thorn which is cropped by the camel,
And then yields him pleasure and nutriment;
When its greenness has gone and it becomes dry,
If the camel crops that same thorn in the desert,
It wounds his palate and mouth without pity,
As if conserve of roses should turn to sharp swords.
When bread is "substance," it is as a green thorn;
When 'tis "form," 'tis as the dry and coarse thorn.
And thou eatest it in the same way as of yore
Thou wert wont to eat it, O helpless being,
Eatest this dry thing in the same manner,
After the real "substance" is mingled with dust;
It has become mingled with dust, dry in pith and rind.
O camel, now beware of that herb!
The Word is become foul with mingled earth;
The water is become muddy; close the mouth of the well,
Till God makes it again pure and sweet;
Yea, till He purifies what He has made foul.
Patience will accomplish thy desire, not haste.
Be patient, God knows what is best.
*NOTES:
1. Muhammadans think the forbidden fruit to have been wheat.
2. The descending node of the moon (see Gulshan i Raz, I. 233).

End of the book.